HUNKA HUNKA
HOWDEE!

POEMS BY RICK LUPERT

MEMPHIS ★ NASHVILLE ★ LOUISVILLE

HUNKA HUNKA
HOWDEE!
⟆POEMS BY RICK LUPERT⟆

Copyright © 2019 by Rick Lupert
All rights reserved

Ain't Got No Press

Design, Layout, Photography ~ Rick Lupert
Author Photo ~ Addie Lupert

First Edition ~ May, 2019

ISBN-13: 978-1-7330278-0-9

Visit the author online at
www.PoetrySuperHighway.com

What did I miss about Memphis? Everything.

- Elvis Presley

Country music is three chords and the truth.

- Harlan Howard

Always carry a flagon of whisky in case of a snake bite, and furthermore, always carry a snake.

- WC Fields

Thank you Addie, Abbie and Feivel, Ellie, Julie, Brendan, Elizabeth, Bill, Corey, Elvis, Johnny, and every duck who ever lived.

The poem *The Mississppi Delta is Shing Like a National Guitar* (page 29) first appeared on Angélique Jamail's blog at www.sapphostorque.com

The cover design is inspired by the historic work of the artists at Hatch Show Print in Nashville, Tennessee. Visit them at www.hatchshowprint.com

To Addie who is my music in every state of the union.

ON THE WAY

Commitments

I don't want to rehash last year's book
but it's two days before our flight to Memphis
and Addie is already scouring the house for
potentially overdue library books so she can
leave California with a clean conscience.

Labels

Addie is in a labeling frenzy
applying Jude's name to every
artifact he is bringing to camp.

She offers to label his playing cards –
all fifty two of them. He politely declines
which sends me into a panic

wondering where I can get
replacement spades and jacks.
As best I can tell they only

come in complete sets –
Like the one we're about to
split up for twelve days.

He'll be on horses and wearing
all-white a couple times a week.
We'll need to leave most of

the bourbon where we found it.
I'm going to put a label on his
forehead and foot.

We can always get another
deck of cards, but this trio
is irreplaceable.

Lyfting

Addie asks me if I have my wedding ring on.
It's been like this ever since that one northeastern debacle
when I didn't.

I'm sitting behind our Lyft driver whose seat is
so far back, the space between my knees and his body
is uncomfortable.

It's good practice for being on the plane
I imagine someone telling me in a comforting manner.
His music is louder than it should be in this situation

and he's already taken us on the wrong freeway.
To be fair, there are those who believe that
all freeways are wrong.

Also we can tell his relationship with the law
may be suspect as the number on his speedometer
is one larger than most legal bodies would prefer.

Yes, I am wearing my wedding ring.
I tell Addie.
Till the day I die.

haiku

Tried to sleep last night
But, apparently, I'm not
very good at it.

Fly's up?

That's my pre-check.

At LAX

I
American runs on Dunkin'.
Who am I to disagree?
Long distance information
get me Memphis, Tennessee.
Or at least get me there,
through Dallas, if necessary.
This coffee, in my cup.
This carry-on, to be carried on.
Gate 46B, my gateway to
the friendly skies.
A salad in my bag
A sugar packet
A fork
Nothing opens before 5am
except my heart.

II
I'm trying to get all
the longer poems in while
I have all this time. Before
the walks from places to
other places mandate
brevity.

III
They try to encourage us
by saying our flight to Dallas is nonstop
which would work if we weren't
headed to Memphis.

IV
The nearby bathrooms are closed
so Addie has to walk to Phoenix
to pee.

V
The people who run the food area
have built a wall of chairs to keep
people out before they open.

VI
The one-item-a-day website
is selling laundry balls and nuts
which leads to far too many uses
of the words *balls* and *nuts*
this early in the morning.

P.S. the balls are supposed to last
for 300 loads.

On The First Plane

I
The pretzels on the floor
from the previous flight
are not helping
anyone's situation.

II
haiku

May it be Your will
that we arrive safely at
our destination

III
Luckily nothing spilled out of
the open salad container, so a
quinoa infested backpack was
not something we were going to
have to worry about.

IV
So much turbulence.
This pilot is probably
in cahoots with our
Lyft driver.

V
I'm not sure of the timing for our connecting flight
and wonder what the best way is to ask the pilot
if he can take surface streets and drop us off
in Memphis before heading to the gate in Dallas.

In Dallas, But Not Really in Dallas

I
Dallas –
So many
connecting
flights. Does
anyone ever
come to
Dallas?

II
Dallas Fort Worth airport
has a penalty box for planes.
Is anyone taking this experience
seriously?

III
I tell Addie *you're allowed to
kill a man in Texas* mainly in
reference to the man who sat
in our aisle and behaved in
an unspeakable manner.

IV
The napkins are huge here
and I look at the woman
who gave it to me and say
"Texas!" holding up
the monstrosity.
"Right?!"
she responds.

V
Speaking of Addie's salad
an unfortunate physics mishap
causes her plastic fork to
catapult over the seat
into the lap of the man
seated in front of me.
For a brief moment
it was like 911
all over again.

WE ARRIVE
IN MEMPHIS

Manifest Duckstiny

It has been decided
that we will see the ducks
this afternoon.

Waiting for the Ducks
at the Peabody

I
You have to get there early or
all you'll see is a *quack*, and

not with your eyes.
I suggest we need to

come back tomorrow with
duck costumes.

Addie says *no* now,
but the night is so young.

II

Kind of Like the Harlem Globetrotters

The Peabody Hotel ducks started in 1933.
I feel it hasn't been the same ducks this whole time.

III
They don't serve duck on
any menu at the Peabody

as per the original contract
with the first duck.

IV
If I were staying at this hotel
I WOULD get a duck disguise

and come down the elevator
five minutes before show time

and scream to all assembled
with my duck bill on

Are you not entertained???

Conversation Between The Peabody Duckmaster and the Ducks While Riding the Elevator Back to the Rooftop Duck Palace

Duckmaster: You guys were great today.
               All day – the quacking, the splashing...
               and you nailed the red carpet back
               to the elevator. The kids loved it!

Ducks: Quack.

Duckmaster: I know!

Two Other Things That Happened in the Peabody Hotel After the Ducks Went Away

I
I dare Addie to run into
the Toyota Marketing Presentation dinner
and yell *Mazda CX-5 motherfuckers!!!!*

(She declines.)

II
We spend an inordinate amount of time
riding the elevator just to hear the sassy
elevator voice say *lobby* over and over.

The Future Mayor

We meet the self-proclaimed future mayor of Memphis
in an art gallery collective space on Main Street.

He scoffs when we tell him we're going to Graceland.
He says they only tell you about Graceland and

Beale Street, and the Civil Rights Museum, and not
the real Memphis. His Memphis...the one of art collectives

and Slave Haven. The one of barbecue joints we couldn't
possibly eat at because of our personal prohibitions.

I tell him there's a reason Niagara Falls is one of the most
visited tourist attractions. It's not because it's popular.

It's because it's awesome. I keep one foot each on and off
the beaten path. I lift what enters both eyes equally high.

I think he sees my point and realizes we did wander
into an arts collective. He wants us to come back for

his *coronation*, though I don't think that's the word he used.
He's got agents in Los Angeles and says he's going to need us.

He is friendly like most people we've met in Memphis.
They rival Ireland with their eagerness to smile.

We smile and walk away towards the famous Beale Street.
Tomorrow we'll meet the King, or at least his ghost.

I haven't slept since the word *Monday* lined our calendars.
My ability to keep my eyes open, has left the building.

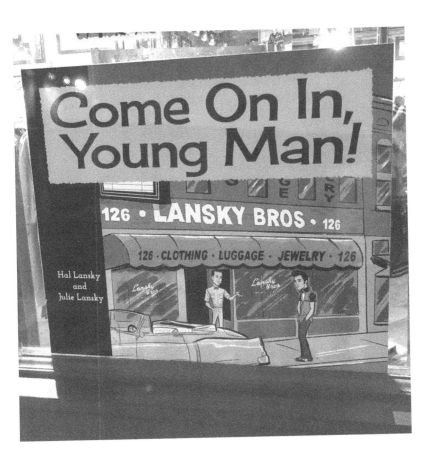

MEMPHIS

DAY ONE

⚡

The Mississippi Delta is Shining Like a National Guitar

I've never woken up in Memphis before and already
there's a hangover of sorts. I'm going to need the day

to flush out Los Angeles. First on the docket is
buying a postcard with a picture of ducks on it.

Second, breakfast at a place that chases the sun.
The amount of humidity is fist fighting with the

available oxygen, and we're putting on *all* the
loose clothing. We're detaching our hair from

our heads. We've got biscuits in our future.
Addie just wants to rock and roll all night, which

is a hell of thing to see this early in the morning.
We *are* going to Graceland.

Shits and Dammits

Addie was full of *shits* and *dammits*
this morning as she checked her email
but the situation resolved itself so
quickly she didn't need to tell me what
it was about, leaving me with a vision
of the cutest "dammit" you've ever seen.

On the Way to Sunrise Cafe

I
A tree and my face become one
on Jefferson Boulevard on the way
to breakfast.

Don't worry. I'm fine.

II
A bird tries to get my attention
I wave but its tweets and cheeps

still seems sad as I get
further away.

At Sunrise Cafe

I
They say, at Sunrise cafe
they have *eggsellent* breakfasts
and they *are not yolking.*
I'm going to sit here and
talk with this sign all day.

II
They serve Stubborn Soda
at Sunrise Cafe though sometimes
the soda refuses.

III
Are you comfortable
I ask Addie in the booths
with the low benches.

By comfortable, do you mean
my butt is sinking into the bench?
Then, yes, I'm great, she responds.

Graceland

I
At first it's quiet like a ghost
then as each foot takes you up

the incline toward the Elvis Pavillion
you start to hear it, in the distance at first

but then like a fog, *Love Me Tender*
arrives in your ears.

There is a reverence to this spectacle
even amidst the ice cream shops and crowds

and jet planes on display. We enter the building
like a dream.

II
We assume this shuttle we are
waiting in line to board will take us
to the mansion, but no one has
said anything. People will stand
in any line.

III
Every where you turn, a snippet
of a song comes out of a bush or
sneaks around a corner. We're so
close to catching him.

IV
A little boy is screaming.
I think he was just told
he's not going to get to
sit on Elvis' lap.

V
Our virtual guide is John Stamos.
Finally I get to spend some quality
time with that guy.

VI
Graceland
is the Disneyland
of Elvis.

VII
We sit down in our traditional
front seats on the shuttle between
the pavilion and the mansion.

VIII
A humble home
relative to what he
could have had.

IX
Priscilla
who still sometimes lives upstairs
says Elvis would rattle down the stairs

X
A carpeted kitchen is
a bold move.

XI
The floor, of course
the walls and the ceiling –
I'm rethinking all the places
I should put carpet.

XII
The jungle room
sometimes a

makeshift
recording studio.

The orange lamp
Priscilla's favorite chair –

The round one.

XIII
Elvis was thirteen when he moved from
Tupelo to Memphis, and that changed
everything for so many people.

XIV
Lisa Marie says Elvis was an avid reader.
I may leave some books by his grave.

XV
Elvis was an official captain
in the Memphis police force.
He would sometimes pull people over,
lecture them about safety and then
send them along with an autograph.
I may get some police lights and start
pulling people over in Van Nuys
and bless them with a poetry reading.
Of course I'll have to wait for them
to rename Sepulveda "Rick Lupert Blvd."

XVI
I rescued a grasshopper
from inside a Graceland bathroom.
That's all right by me.

XVII
I can't help but tear up at the grave
of the man I never met, and in a way
I just met. Oh the people who've
impacted our lives whose hands we've
never shaken. I'm all shook up.

XVIII
We declined the $35 photo package
but Addie says *it's okay, we'll always have
the memory of you manhandling me.*

XIX
Elvis
Took
Care
of
Business

XX
The Elvis archives include
many of his personal possessions

including an illustrated yoga book,
A TV with a gunshot through the screen,

luggage, boxing gloves, everything gold,
police badges, binoculars, *the* microphone,

a ticket to one of his own concerts, an amplifier,
a phonograph, another amplifier (there were more),

old telephones, new telephones, plaques, Bibles,
and then I ran out of time to write it all down.

But one thing's for sure, when I get home,
I'm carpeting everything.

XXI
John Lennon said *Before Elvis there was nothing*.
I've seen history books that prove otherwise, but
he may have just been referring to himself, musically.

XXII
We eat french fries at Gladys' –
Not cooked by the original Gladys.

XXIII
I can only imagine the staff here hears
every refrain of *Love Me Tender*
so often, that a daily orgy of violent
carnage ensues as they start killing
each other when it comes on. (So much.)

XXIV
Poster Phrases

Elvis invaded
the land of the bikinis.

Elvis – feudin' lovin' singin'.
Swinging higher than the Space Needle!

Elvis is kissin' cousins again,
and also friends, and friends of friends,

and even some perfect strangers.
He's playing *Indian* but he doesn't say

how, he says *when!*
With his foot on the gas

and no brakes on the fun.
Torrid together, singing, dancing,

turning on the romance
as they make the speed scene

at the famed furious Charlotte 600.
Smooth, fast and in high gear!

I slipped, I stumbled, I fell,
It's all about young people

and their growing pains.
The heat from the desert,

the laughs from everyone,
the beats from town.

The trouble with girls
(how to get into it).

XXV
Before anyone did anything,
Elvis did everything.

XXVI
One of Elvis' costume designers
was named Nudie Cohen.

I just think it's funny that someone
who dressed people was named *Nudie.*

XXVII
Addie wants to touch Elvis' brown faux-fur suit
which is in a glass case. So I lift my hands in the air
and gesture for someone to come over.
As is the custom for all people when they encounter me,
nothing happens.

Hoppers Unite

The *Hop In* convenience store
is where Addie would do all her shopping.
When I tell her this she smiles and says
Yes...yes.

At Sun Studios

I
Rock and roll isn't about rules
but the tour guide has some for us
anyway.

II
Rufus M. Gordon, Jr....
and his rooster, Butch,
recorded here.

III
Another beautiful mistake –
Stuffed newspaper inside
a broken amplifier led to
distortion.

IV
Hound Dog was originally
a song called
Bear Cat...

V
Elvis' first recording was a
sweet ballad for his mother.
Elvis loved his mother more
than I ever could.

VI
Elvis' high school yearbook
behind a glass case –
Everyone in high school
in the forties, looked a hundred
years older than they do today.

VII
Sam Phillips was always looking for
perfect imperfection.

VIII
A lot of people kiss the X where Elvis stood
and our guide encourages us to do the same.
He says he's done it himself. He is a musician
and has the appropriate reverence for the ground
upon which he stands.

Addie is a Lumberjack, or a Tree

The ever adaptable Addie is now proclaiming *timber*
every time she spontaneously leans over into me
when she's tired, or just needs to get to the floor
to do some stretching. This started a couple of days ago
after I stated *timber* when she first fell in my direction.

Warzone

Parts of Memphis are completely destroyed
and with no activity in these shells of buildings,
whose ceilings have collapsed on stairways,
we're not sure if they're being repaired or in a
permanent state of disrepair. The war is here,
or came and never left. Sometimes I wonder
where I am.

I Say Things to Addie in the Streets of Memphis

I
Addie asks what's happening
at the Fedex forum where a
large crowd is gathered.
Everyone's just waiting for packages
I assure her. You'll have to ask her
If she believed me.

II
Addie sees a sign for the Fire Museum
and asks *what's that.* I tell her *no one knows
since it burned down.*

Addie is having a war of words with the talking elevator.

Alright give me your angriest 'ground'
she demands, and let me tell you
she is not happy with the results.
The ground floor couldn't come
soon enough as the doors open
and we head off to dinner.

At South of Beale

I
The rosemary
going up your nose
when you drink
is a nice touch.

II
We work really hard to position
the glass so the rosemary does
look like it's going up my nose
so the photo and the poem
are legitimate.

I'm a cicada whisperer

I say to Addie as,
for the second time tonight,
all the cicadas in a tree
stop making their cicada noise
when I walk by.

At Beale Sweets Sugar Shack

The candy store on Beale Street
has Willie Wonka (the original)
playing in permanent rotation
on their TV, which is a beacon
of sensibility to candy store TV
owners everywhere.

Languatory

The nearby Chisca Hotel
should not be pronounced
shiksa hotel under any
circumstances.

Beale Street

is not
Bourbon Street.
But,
to be fair,
the reverse
is also
true.

The Heavy King

I'd like to sum up my day in words
different from the ones you've already read.

But my feet have gone out of business
and my head feels like it's going bankrupt

and my stomach is permanently closed
and the light switches on the other side

of the room aren't going to turn themselves off.
I can tell you this – I met the King today.

I know what he did, and where he slept.
I know where he bought his clothes, and

in a sense,
I met the man who clothed him.

I saw his cars and jumpsuits and
would have touched every one

if it weren't for the signs.
His peanut butter and racketballs

His ceramic monkeys and airplanes
Almost every one of his possessions.

Someone else's life is a heavy weight
to carry through the day.

Good evening, Memphis. And goodnight.
I'll meet your other King tomorrow.

One quick final note:

At Doubletree hotels
you're entitled to the

free chocolate chip cookies
they give you at check-in

anytime you want
during your stay and

not just at check-in.
This changes

EVERYTHING!

A clarification on the previous "final" note:

Just to be clear, when I said "final note"
on the previous page, I just meant final for today.

A further clarification:

Just to be clear, when I said "today"
on the previous page, I meant the day that
I was writing these poems, which was
June 21, 2018. I fully acknowledge that
you are likely reading this on a
completely different day.

A Final Note:

We can't go on like this.

MEMPHIS
DAY TWO

Walking to Breakfast

There's a sign on top of a building that says "Flying Saucer"
which isn't near any restaurant or store called "Flying Saucer"

so I'm not sure if it's meant as a warning to the populace
or as an inviting message to outer space.

In any case further down the block I see
a bar called "Flying Saucer" which invalidates

this entire train of thought.
I'm sorry for wasting your time.

Walking to breakfast

hand in hand with my beloved
a man wonders how we did it.

How did two people the exact same height
find each other? I tell him *I had myself*

*shortened by three inches before
our wedding.*

Alright he says.
Had to do it I say.

At the National Civil Rights Museum

"...say that I was a drum major for justice...
say that I was a drum major for righteousness..."

~ Dr. Martin Luther King, Jr.

Give Me Pause

Missing commas on the first display
cause us to spend an extra several minutes
figuring out what it means to say.
I'm happy for the extra time in this place,
but I do want to make an extra donation
to get them some punctuation.

Names

This is for Kunta Kinte and
the other 12 and a half million Africans.
This is for Larry Payne
This is for Elias Clayton
Elmer Jackson
Isaac McGhie
Earl Little
Medgar Evers
Herbert Lee
Mack Parker
Clinton Melton
Lamar Smith
Emmett Till
James Chaney
Andrew Goodman
Michael Schwerner
Cynthia Dianne Wesley
Reverend George Lee
Col. Roman Ducksworth, Jr.
Walter Harris
Jimmy Lee Jackson
Viola Liuzzo

This is for the one dollar an hour sanitation workers
This is for Loren Catherine Bailey
Yitzhak Rabin
Harvey Milk
Anwar Sadat
for anyone uprooted,
lynched, shot down,
made to feel *less*.

This is for Matthew Shepard.
This is for Martin.

This is for a book with
just names, every name.

Feel free...

They built in a room
where people sing together
songs of freedom
like *Ain't Gonna Let Nobody
Turn Me Around* and
Which Side Are You On?
Feel free to sing along
the sign says.

Walking Through the Museum

I
We listen to every word
of Martin's speech in Washington.
Every word.

II
A woman with skin picks up a red phone
and says she's talking with the president.
I tell her to say *hi* for me
She says *it's not Trump.*
And I say *good*, she should
hang up if it was.

III
Martin's last words –
I want you to play it real pretty
spoken to Ben Branch
Precious Lord

IV
There is poetry in protest
in mountaintops in Selma
There is poetry in freedom riders
and bus riders, in promised lands
There is poetry in colors and desegregation
in underground railroads
There is poetry in *I am a man*

V
Elvis died at 42
Martin Luther King at 39
I'm already 49 and haven't
accomplished a toenail's worth
of what either did.

VI
I'll be on the Carpet of Unity
tired Addie says in the lobby
of the legacy building.

Inappropriate

Addie rejects my idea to
leave the leftover food from breakfast
that we hoped to give to a hungry person
in the lounge at the Civil Rights Museum
with a sign on it that says *Free at Last.*

Stolen Tongues

In the car on the way to the next place
we hear, on the radio, a New Zealand man
stole two human tongues. It's not clear if he
took them from inside two mouths
or from a local repository of tongues.

At the Bass Pro Pyramid

I
We're in the camouflage clothing section of the
Bass Pro Shop inside a giant pyramid which, for us,
is the only attraction (Certainly it isn't the acre of
ammunition not to mention the items that house
ammunition) and Addie says *I've never seen so
many different kinds of ammunition* to which I
respond *or have you?*

II
Right next to the guns is the *Unlimited Ducks
Waterfowl Heritage Center.* So *to the left* if you
want to kill ducks, and *to the right* if you want to
celebrate their lives. We're heading to a vegan
restaurant to cleanse ourselves of this.

Lyfting

We think Lyft drivers set the volume of their music
based on whether or not they want to interact with you.
All we could tell *Mamadou* was how much we liked
his seat decorations before we were drowned out
all the way to the vegan restaurant.

What I Saw

Today I saw the spot where Martin was shot
and the spot where he was shot from.

I saw a tunnel to a cellar where slaves
crawled for their lives. I saw free men

catapult themselves down Beale Street
for nothing more than whatever I was

willing to put in a bucket. I saw buckets.
I saw rocks made of ice. I saw a two dollar

duck and kept it forever unlike at
the Absinthe Room where it was

two dollars just to walk into the room.
I saw smiles and flowers and a piano

that sang with no one's hands.
I saw banjos from Africa. A bridge

for human feet only that spanned
the entire Mississippi. I saw a pyramid

my ancestors had nothing to do with.
I saw it all. I saw it all.

It's a Condition

What are you drinking?
Addie asks two women on Beale Street

holding oversized plastic champagne bottles
with giant straws.

You can get any drink you want in this
for twenty five dollars, and I got a Virgin for twelve.

I always thought a Virgin would cost a lot more
I say.

You do realize you are saying the things you think
out loud, don't you? Addie says.

Actually I think she said that about my comment about
Blind Mississippi Morris playing at the club when I said,

in what I imagined to be his voice, *can someone*
move the mic in front of my face, I can't see!

MEMPHIS
DAY THREE

Quackxploitation

Addie puts the two dollar rubber ducky garnish
that came with last night's drink inside her backpack.
I'm not sure if me, or Memphis, are ready for what
that means for us today.

At Tamp & Tap

I
It didn't take long at breakfast
before the duck came out which
made up a little bit for the absence
of the bluegrass band the restaurant's
website promised.

II
He wants to know if I
want to keep my fork and
I glance at Addie's frittata
and say *you never know
what might happen.
That's what I'm talking
about* he says as he
heads back to the kitchen
with just my saucer.

III
I'm about to start
my own bluegrass brunch
up in this Tamp & Tap.

IV
I decide to improvise an
instrumentless bluegrass brunch
for the couple that came in
after us.

Addie is suspicious
of this effort at first, but
eventually joins in
with percussion.

Too bad I didn't have my
long pants with me as I could
have done my jig of straightening
out the bottoms.

I'm just working for tips
ladies and gentleman.

Identify The Key Syllables in This Poem

The sign says Jodi Rump is a dentist
but I think she should be an assist.

Notes From the Cotton Museum

I
Memphis is the wellspring
from which modern music
was born.

II
I notice the raw cotton
kind of looks like cotton balls –
and another vital connection
of common sense is established.

III
The observations are coming
quickly and by the time I tell Addie
we should plant some cotton
in our back yard, she really wants
me to slow down, but I'm already
on to where I can buy Jude appropriate
clothing for picking cotton.

IV
The earliest known cotton plant
emerged sixty-five million years ago.
This will remain true no matter what
century of human existence
in which you read this.

V
We sit in the original chairs used
in the Cotton Exchange...those
long gone souls never imagined
an introductory video.

VI
*Should I leave my
clothes here as a tribute*
is a question no one is
willing to answer.

VII
Cotton married blues
to country and rock
and roll was born.

VIII
I'm already imagining
all the money I'll save
on cotton balls after
I harvest my lone
backyard cotton plant.

IX
The sign says *take a look*
hovers over a perpetually blank screen.
I'm not sure what I've accomplished here.

X
The shirts in the gift shop
are not 100% cotton.
Come on Cotton Museum
you had one job...

Street Thoughts

I
There's a store on Union Avenue
called "Unofficial" which is hard
to take seriously.

II
Business names permanently
carved into buildings –
Their owners never imaging
the impermanence of it all.

III
It occurs to me that
Evils and *Elvis*
are just a traveling
I apart.

Back at the Peabody Hotel Where We Are Not Staying But We Sure Like Hanging Out In

I
They have baby changing stations
at the Peabody Hotel.
If I had a baby, I wouldn't know
what if change it into.

II
We go to see the ducks in the lobby fountain
but we hear Mr. Duck was misbehaving
and had to stay in the rooftop palace.

III
Yes,
I ended the title of this poem
with a preposition.
Fight me.

Sunglasses at Lansky 126

(a found poem)

Gardening with a Kraken
Swedish meatball hangover

Phoenix at a bloody mary bar
Whiskey shots with Satan

Peeping Tom's dino fetish
Requiem for a longneck

Mud wrestling with Nedry
Not the mama

Sunbathing with wizards
Iced by yetis

Flamingos on a booze cruise
Messi's midnight orgy

Vincent's absinthe night terrors
Donkey goggles

Going to Valhalla...
Witness!

I think they're trying pretty hard
to come up with a Rick Lupert
book title.

Meatitude

Pig on Beale Street advertises
"pork with an attitude."
Hi. I'm a hotdog, and fuck you.

Notes from the Gibson Factory Tour

He tells us, even the smallest imperfection
will send an unfinished product to *Guitar Heaven*.

I am soon forbidden from asking questions
but I don't remember why.

I also don't remember what the CNC machine does.
Someone asks (maybe me, but it doesn't sound
like something I would ask).

Where do you source wood from?
Trees he answers.

Someone wrote *fart* on the container that stores
the markers on the guitar wall for *tourees* to sign.

He refuses to tell me what the "F" in *F Hole* stands for
and I know he heard my question.

May your F holes ever resonate.
he tells us.

At the Rock 'n' Soul Museum

I
The woman selling tickets at the Rock N Soul Museum
didn't believe me when I told her we were both eight.
Thank God for the Triple A discount.

II
In the early fifties the races were reaching for each other
and in Memphis it was happening before our eyes.

III
I wrote *spirit of the blackness.*
for some reason.

IV
Rock and Roll was
a black and white project
invented in Memphis.

V
He'd knock you down quicker
than a wild cat licker
are some of the lyrics from
Mule Boogie which you should
go listen to right now.

VI
Mississippi Bo Weavil Blues
by Charlie Patton too.

VII
Beale Street wasn't a tourist thing
like it is now. It was a way of life.

VIII
At white owned WDIA
the black announcers
were not allowed to touch the knobs
and turn the dials. But when
the white engineer's girlfriend
would come along he would
disappear and someone would
have to adjust the potentiometers.

IX
They'd make public service announcements
on the radio, like about a farmer's missing cow,
or a man's missing teeth. *Man can't eat,
he ain't got no teeth* the DJ would say.

X
WHER was the first all-girl radio station.
Every 'girl' when hired at the beginning

thought they were going to be the
only one there.

*This is WHER...and now the news
from a-broad.*

XI
Dewey Phillips on WHBQ in Memphis
was the first DJ to play Elvis on the radio.
Tell 'em Phillips sent ya he'd say.

XII
I'm re-listening to the lyrics of *Soul Man*
and trying to figure out how to incorporate
this into a worship service.

XIII
Isaac Hayes' *By the time I get to Phoenix*
was the first spoken word song
as far as I'm concerned.

XIV
"Hi Records" –
Well, hello there!

XV
Hi Records was succeeded by
a company called *How Ya Doin' Records*
and exists today as
I'm Fine, Thanks, Studios.

XVI
I press the numbers 2, 8, and 0
to hear *Theme from Shaft.*
You're damn right, I'm going to
remember these numbers.

At Blues City Cafe

I
Blind Mississippi Morris
is accompanied by
Bald Down the Middle New Jersey Fred
Tiger Woods Lookalike Nashville Steve
and Fully Bald Arkansas Kareem Abdul Jabaar

II
I see two people sitting at the
3 or more table. Blind Mississippi Morris
can smell that kind of evil.

III
Blind Mississippi Morris
could have been B.B. King
or any of them.

He *is* Beale Street
once a day, every day
born and bred.

Mouth on the harp –
The wind that comes
out of his mouth

butterflies from
a hundred years ago.

IV
Blind Mississippi Morris
can't do it by himself.

He's not sure if that's your man
He's not sure if that man had a shotgun.

You've got to help him.
Don't make him find someone else.

He's just playing that harmonica
        to release his pain.
This hurts so much, like it should.

Put something in his love bucket
He'll be back in thirty minutes.

V
I've been drinking
this beer so long
I don't know which way
is oop.

Overheard in A. Schwab's Dry Goods Store on Beale Street

I'm not going to get the elephant.
I can get the elephant somewhere else.

I don't want Elvis.
I want Memphis.

I am not your friend.
I'll be your friend

I don't see anything I want to try.
We'll be here all night.

My blues name is

Skinny Fingers Parker
in case you wanted to know.

Nightcap at the Peabody Lobby Bar

I
Ducks long since asleep –
we save two dollars by
bringing our own
rubber ducky garnish.

II
Most of the way through the cocktail
I forget to involve my mouth and start
to pour the drink, and have to rush my
head over to receive the beverage.

MEMPHIS TO NASHVILLE

Is This It, Memphis?

The all night party in the room next door
finally ended and we were able to get a
solid fifteen minutes of sleep.

I'd like to blame the revelers but
if you're leaving a city, you should be
awake for most of your final moments.

We're crossing the street for breakfast
with a family of righteous individuals.
We'll get to see the ducks one last time.

Do you get nostalgic reading this
like I do writing it? Are you imagining
their feathers, their little duck eyes

looking at you, heartbroken you
may never see them again? Oh Nashville
what will you do to make up for this?

Back at the Peabody for Breakfast

I
There's the *Frank Schutt Room*
off the second floor of the lobby.
I just want to tell him to
Schutt the Frank up.

II
They have a piano made for
Frances Scott Key up here.
Revolutionary, anthem writer,
lived well into the 1800's.
His Keyes covered in glass now
with *Do Not Touch* reminding us
what America has become.

III
We question the legitimacy
of the Elvis impersonator in the lobby
when Addie notices his cape is stuffed
under his belt. *Still alive...still alive*
he says to anyone who will listen
whoever he is.

IV
Autocorrect wants to change
Elvis to Alexa. My phone
misses Seattle.

V
Everyone wants to
sit on Elvis' lap. He is the
Memphis Santa.

Feivel Tells Me About Bluffs

In particular, Memphis is on a bluff
and Arkansas, across the river,
lies below and doesn't do so well
when it floods.

Feivel's wife is Abbie who we know
from the sacred place. She sings like
tomorrow has been cancelled.

Their daughter and son are
cuter than all the ducks.
One of them wears polka dots, and
if you ask them for a hug,
it may not happen.

Driving Music Highway to Nashville

I
Even the GPS doesn't want us to leave Memphis.
It pretends to not know where we are after we pick up the rental car.
We have to drive slow so we don't end up in Arkansas.

II
A sign says *Turn signals,*
the original instant message.
This is the kind of sensibility that
makes me want to move to a place.

III
Another sign tells us we are on the
Isaac Hayes Memorial Highway.
Out of respect, we're shutting our mouths
all the way to Nashville.

IV
We're entering the Loosahatchie River Watershed.
Finally! I can search for my loose hatchi that I lost
in the river.

V
Auto correct wants to change *Loosahatchie*
to *head cheese* which fills me with all the emotions.

VI
The signs tell us the road is *grooved*.
We wouldn't expect anything less
from *Music Highway.*

Ross in Phoenix Makes an Appearance

I receive an emergency poetry request
from Ross in Phoenix while we're waiting
for our room to be ready in Nashville.

He's taking a group of people to Israel
tomorrow and needs a poem for them to
read on the plane.

When I say *tomorrow* I mean the tomorrow
specific to today, the day I'm writing this,
and not the tomorrow of when you're

reading this, which I suspect are
completely different days. I'm able to
accommodate with an appropriate

set of words and, now, somehow,
Ross in Phoenix has made it into my
book of poems from the mid-south.

Glancing at Restaurants on Google Maps

They have a *Wild Cow, Wild Eggs,*
and a *Wild Beaver Saloon* here.
If only our room were ready here
at the Wild Doubletree, we could
put almost anything in our mouths.

It's Called the Cumberland

Our Lyft driver didn't know the
name of the river running through her town.
I can't imagine going anywhere without
the name of the local water spitting
out of my tongue.

On Broadway

At first glance
Broadway is the
Champs-Élysées
of Beale Streets.

At Bakersfield
(Not the one in California)

I
We arrive at a restaurant called *Bakersfield*
which doesn't exactly make me feel at home.

II
Somehow the phrase
hard corn is said by the waiter.
I giggle and say *hard corn*.
He sees what I did there.

III
In another failure of my ability to
navigate the laws of physics
I try to push the table closer to Addie,
but it's already as far as it goes and
I end up pushing myself away from the table.

A Concern

I wonder if the Indigo Girls
stay at the Hotel indigo when
they're in town and if they
get a discount.

A Fact

Morris Frank
from Nashville
was blind in 1914
like Blind Mississippi Morris
from Memphis is
in 2018.

A Cautionary Tale

The corner of our hotel is sharp
so we avoid rubbing our bodies
against it.

I Can Feel It

I remember Rodney at Gibson Guitar in Memphis
sniffling as he handed me a *house guitar pick*.
Now, a day later, I lay in bed in Nashville
with a sore throat. I'm prepared to take *NyQuil*
and *DayQuil*, and any other kind of *Quil* that
will prevent the impedance of this experience.
From music city to music city, nothing can
prevent Kentucky's Bourbon from becoming
a part of my D.N.A.

Art Tomorrow

The kind on walls.
Not the kind on Garfunkels.
But who am I to say
what art is?

NASHVILLE
DAY ONE

A Few Morning Quickies

I
I'm all for collecting and redeeming points
but the Hilton HHonors tote bag feels like
it would be too much of a public display
of allegiance.

II
The Tennessee State Museum next door
to our hotel is closed for relocation.
Maybe if I walk around with a
Hilton Honors tote bag, the concierge
will give me the keys so we can
develop a private tour of the
hollowed out shell of Tennessee.

III
Juan drives us to breakfast.
I want to walk around Nashville
with a Juan branded tote bag.

At Milk & Honey

We're sitting at the silver bar
with an excellent view of the sous-chefs.

One woman chops kale the entire time we're there
which has Addie considering a career move.

There's no talking to her once the baker
takes the bread out of the oven and

starts stacking it on a shelf next to my head.
The largest bag of rice flour is

sitting next to me. Our view of eggs
is replaced by bags of meat.

That's our cue to
head to the museum.

At the Frist Art Museum

I
Waiting for the Barbarians
Neo Rauch, 2007

If I were a barbarian
I'd want to meet the guy
with the pointy orange face too.

II
A mother wheels her baby into
the first gallery. Her eyes are wider
than Broadway. She smiles at me
like we're both monkeys who've
discovered the golden banana
and it's ours forever.

III
Winchester
Jeremy Blake, 2002

We enter the room of abstract
video images and ominous sound.
Addie takes a seat. A slow blur from
one to the next. Audible flickering
like film. We leave when the silhouette
of the man with a rifle shows up.

IV
Birds
Ahmed Alsoudani, 2015

This one's called *Birds*
but it's the hanging eyeballs
that draw me in.

V
But a Storm is Blowing from Paradise
Rokni Haerizadeh, 2014

The shark in the lower left panel
looks like a man in a shark costume.

VI
Revolution 2.0- RFGA
Ghada America and Reza Farkhondeh, 2011

Do you know how much I want to touch that
Addie asks about this one.
Yes, yes I do.

VII
The Egyptian Lover
Ghada Amer, 2008

Both behind a mesh so
no one sees when she takes
Snow White's innocence.

VIII
Funkalicious fruit field
Wangechi Muru, 2007

Features a star child
flying over a field of boots
using a mothership
of her own creation.

IX
Love Story
Ghost Story
Afruz Amighi, 2018

Addie doesn't see much difference
between the *love story* and the
ghost story. *Did you see the movie*
Ghost, I ask her. Yes, she answers.
I didn't I tell her which sends her
into a conniption of disbelief, adding
yet another film to her list of movies
she can't believe I haven't seen.

X
4 Headdresses
Afruz Amighi, 2017

Headdress for the Unborn:
With feathers so they'll
have a nice place to land

Fool's Headdress:
Fool got an arrow
shot through his head.

Warrior's Headdress:
You don't want to get into
a war with a guy that looks
like that.

Headdress for the Beheaded:
It's nice that someone's thinking of
the beheaded.

XI
Untitled
Wade Guyton, 2005

The giant U in the middle of the painting
stands for untitled.

XII
Semiosis on the Sea
James Perrin, 2015

And they've brought their colored pencils with them!

XIII
Over the Sky of the Beyond
Kazuki Umezawa, 2014

Addie spots the ducky
in this complex painting
with a joyful *there's a ducky!*

XIV
And now it's all about
strategic maneuvering so I'm
not standing next to the man
who hasn't showered
since the Civil War.

XV
All the "please do not touch" signs
are under the plaques describing
the art, which leads me to believe
I can touch the art all I want.

XVI
The sparkle in Addie's eye
tells me the answer to her
question *"can we go see the
children's hands on area"*
is going to be *"yes"*.

Lyfting

We drive by the *Just Love* coffeehouse
which makes us wonder if they even
serve coffee there.

At Belmont Mansion

I
We visit Joseph and Adelicia's
tête-à-tête room. Now Addie
and I have to put one of these in
back in Van Nuys.

II
Ruth, the statue,
has always been
in the house.

III
Adelicia Acklen
went on a statue
shopping spree.

IV
*Is this the original fake display chicken
in the dining room* I decline to ask our guide
who has made it clear that's not the kind of question
she would tolerate.

V
Necessaries de Voyage
Oh, Joseph Acklen...your toiletries kit
is not as portable as my 2018 sensibility
would want it to be.

VI
I'm heartbroken to find out
Adelicia's name is not *Addielicious*
as I've been hearing it this whole time.

VII
I bring out my fancy voice to declare
our intentions to dine here tonight,
only to discover a much more fancy
formal dining room across the hall, and
realize my efforts have been wasted.

VIII
Our tour guide refuses to tell me if
descendants of the Acklens get
free admission to the tour.

IX
After Adelicia sold the house
they started putting up buildings
willy-nilly.

Cornerfest Destiny

We take the traditional photograph of
me walking into a corner and Addie says
"You didn't really need to *thunk* into the corner"
referring to the noise made when I pressed my
body up against the intersecting walls.
"Didn't I, Addie? Didn't I?"

The Belmont University Quad

used to be Adelicia Acklen's front yard –
The water tower now a bell tower
The live animals for the public to view
      replaced with bronze statues.
The Gazebo hasn't changed much.
The bell strikes *five* –
But the mansion gets its water
      another way now.

Grassumption

A family of three squirrels eats
off the Belmont University Quad lawn.
Or maybe they're just friends?

In Front of the Jack C. Massey College of Business

If you look at it quick the signs appears to say
The Jack Ass College of Business.

At Gray and Dudley

Despite the hanging animal sculptures
in this museum / hotel / restaurant
we are quickly befriended by Laura
the server, singer and *Nashvillian*.
She is the one you want as an
emissary to your food.

We Spent the Day

We spent the day with art
and old guitars and pretending
not to be sick. A giant apple

made an appearance. We spent
the day with facial tissue in our
pockets and in cars that came

when buttons were pressed.
We heard no music in Music City
today, though we're sure it was there.

We spent the day with our eyes
and only touching certain things.
We spent the day with Ellie from

the sacred place and a giant
penguin. Several giant penguins
if you must know. We were all

surprised when the giant meerkat
showed up in the lobby, or rather
we showed up in the lobby and

he was already there. We spent the
day wondering if other apples
were available, and in elevators

and talking with the real decision makers.
We spent the day wondering where

then ten pound weights had gone.
(We weren't the only ones...)
We spent the day in all three

dimensions, in Nashville where
we can afford to spend
two days more.

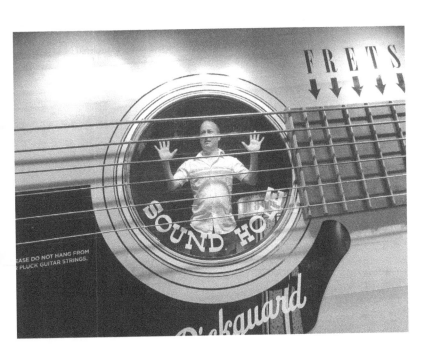

NASHVILLE

DAY TWO

What I Remember, This Morning

So much has happened since
my eyes opened at eight o'clock
and my arrival at this restaurant.
But I'm forgetting most of it
because this carrot bread couldn't
be any more legitimate. I know
for sure my mouth opened and
the carrot bread went inside.
I have a vague memory of
handing a postcard to a woman
named *Keeley* who made promises
that all efforts would be made to
transport it to our blonde offspring
on the west coast. I remember
getting in a Toyota driven by
a man who wouldn't say much.
I'm confident I dragged a brush
across my teeth and, I'm not sure
I even want to tell you this, but
I pressed a hot iron up against
a buttoned down shirt. It is the
fourteenth anniversary of the day
we put on the black and white
Chinese outfits of our love.
Now they call that *appropriation*.
This is everything I remember.

Little Mosko's

describes itself as
a *muncheonette*.
There's an unexpected
lack of munchkins
eating here.

Applerition

We discover on
the side of a coffee cup

the words *Addie*
and *apple*, look almost

the same.
Addie –

the apple
of my eyes.

In Disguise

I'm dressed like I
might like country music.
So, I'm hoping to blend right in
at the Country Music Hall of Fame.

Everybody Calm Down

Addie says she's getting ready to strip.
It's not what you think. It's just hot outside
and some layers need to come off.

Kabrunch!

I could have done without the explosion
during brunch. I understand sometimes
you have to blow up buildings but
couldn't it happen after the meal?

There is construction everywhere.
They're building a new Nashville.
We have hardly had the chance
to meet the old one.

Would you like some broken fragments of a fluorescent light

I ask Addie as we pass some
on Peabody Street, not because
I think she'll say *yes*, I just want
to be polite.

P.S. This didn't really happen.

Always Biscuits

Kitchen Notes on 4th Street
at Korean Veterans Boulevard
has a sign that says *We serve
biscuits all day.*

Honey, this is where I will be
all day.

At the Country Music Hall of Fame and Museum

I
Our tickets say we are customer number 0.
They're already onto us.

II
The elevator to the third floor shakes
but, appropriately, it does not
rattle or roll.

III
Now I see holes
everywhere.

IV
Country music is rooted in the
folk traditions of the British Isles.
Everything is connected to
the very beginning.

V
They had to provide for
their own amusements
down by the railroad
in the Blue Ridge Mountains.

VI
The choreographed 1929
Oh Susana by the Blue Ridgers
with Cordelia Mayberry –
Not too far from the posses
accompanying 2018's
hip hop performers.

VII
I hear Paul Warmack
and his Gully Jumpers
really shredded back
in the day.

VIII
Addie likes the mustache guitars.
Enough said.

IX
Roy Acuff originated celebrity food branding
with his *own* sacks of flour blend.

X
Merle Travis helped turn
Capitol Records into a
country music powerhouse
with his hit *Divorce Me C.O.D.*

XI
Hard Country –
It's like hard rock
except without
the rock.

XII
Elvis Presley had
a solid gold Cadillac
among many, many
other things.

XIII
Hee Haw –
Bless your pea brained
cotton pickin' hearts.

XIV
Someone get me a Kleenex –
I think I'm catching
hillbilly fever.

XV
I'm as confused as they are about what
a *Plectrum Paganini* is.

XVI
I'm giving it all up
to start a jug band.
Can someone please
send me a jug?

XVII
Johnny Cash and Bobby Dylan –
Looking into each other's eyes
singing *True Love of Mine*.

At Historic RCA Studio B

I
Debbie says *wave* if
you can't hear her.
She promises
to wave back.

II
Uncle Dave Macon
was the Grandfather of
country music

*Welcome to the
Grand ole Opry*
he'd say.

III
We're
Heading to
Music Row

IV
Debbie says the fine print
on our tickets is a recording contract.
I've never been more ready for this.

V
RCA Studio B –
Home of a thousand hits
Debbie makes us
sing *Yesterday* together
She is awed by the power
of our voices.

Plus I think we just
put fifty bucks in
Paul McCartney's pocket.

VI
Debbie is convinced that
songs recorded here
stayed in the walls.

VII
Elvis recorded forty-four hits
in this room, and a total of
two hundred thirty songs.
(Do the math)

VIII
You know how I love being
in places where things happened –
Here in Studio B I can hear all
the things that happened.

IX
There is a power
in this room where
iconic riffs were birthed.

X
This is where they
dropped the twang to
create the *Nashville sound.*

XI
Two songs that battled to the death here
were *What's He Doing in My World?*
and *Welcome to My World.*

XII
The hung blanket was
the first isolation booth.
It saved Roy Orbison's Career
(as the instruments were
drowning him out.)

XIII
*I'd like to do it one more time
and hold the last note just
a little bit longer.*
        ~ Jim Reeves.

XIV
It's our wedding anniversary
so when Dolly Parton singing
I Will Always Love You starts
here in the room where it
was recorded, it doesn't take
half a glance at Addie's eyes
for water to start coming
out of mine.

XV
We take photos at
Elvis' favorite piano.
Thank you Elvis.

XVI
Debbie tells us to hold on to our rock socks
when *Lucky Penny* comes on.
I feel my socks are insufficient
for this request.

XVII
I thank my lucky stars
I am not lonesome tonight.

XVIII
RCA shut the studio down
when Elvis died.

XIX
Debbie tells us we are the best group
and she's *not just saying that*.
She definitely made us feel
like the best.

XX
Once, when Elvis was signing contracts
in Los Angeles, fans outside started to
tear apart his car. The security guard told him
they were going to arrest everyone.
Elvis told him to *let them all go.*
But Elvis, they've torn apart your whole car.
There's nothing left. Elvis said again
let them all go...they paid for it.

Back at the Museum

I
The last thing I want to do
is to have Loretta Lynn take me
on a trip to *Fist City.*

II
Loretta was given an army jacket
with the rank *combat country singer*
when she toured with the USO.
If only all wars were fought
with country music.

III
We see video of Willie Nelson
clean cut, in a suit and tie
before he discovered the doobie
and let his hair grow to Memphis.

IV
We gave Nashville an illusion of literacy.
People said Kris and I were the only people
who could describe Dolly Parton without
using our hands.
> ~ Tom T Hall

V
The only things Willie Nelson saved
from his burning Nashville house in 1970
were his Martin Guitar and his
trash bag full of marijuana.

VI
Pairing outlaws and armadillos
in one exhibit, has been a boon to the
street-cred of armadillos.

VII
A song ain't nothin' in the world but a
story just wrote with music.
                ~ Hank Williams

VIII
The circle
will remain
unbroken.

Hatch Show

We tour the Hatch Show gallery
and print shop where they tell us
advertising without posters
is like fishing without worms and
negative space is held with furniture.
We operate a printing press.
We take our posters home.
We cover our poetry books with
what they taught us.

Don't let me leave without telling you about the boots.

And the hats.

Home Cooked Breakfast

One restaurant says they offer
home cooked breakfast.
I believe they cook the food at home
then drive it here to the restaurant.
Addie believes they live here.

Walking the Pedestrian Bridge

Time to throw my phone into the
Cumberland River.

Beware!

We've seen this woman twice on Broadway
asking if we'd like a carriage ride –
no horses or carriages in sight.
Beware the *machete carriage ride
stranglerette* of Nashville.

At Benchmark on 2nd

I'm not superstitious but
the song he's playing is.

She wants us to give him
a hand, so we give him

all our hands. This is our
anniversary weekend on

2nd Avenue. It was either
here or the uncertainty of

a rooftop. One acoustic
guitar and two voices

made the decision easy.
They're out of the local

brew, so I start to train
my bourbon sensibility

with an ale from across
the border. The waitress

wants to know if she
should start a tab.

I tell her *no* as *I'm a
one drink a day kind*

*of guy, and this is
already my second.*

It may be time to
stop defining my

line lengths by
how wide my phone is.

They ask if there are
any requests and then

play other songs
claiming to not remember

what was requested.
Ross, the guitarist,

says he's on the wagon
but drinks all the gifted

shots. *Tipping is sexy*
the jar in front of them

beckons. This whole
night in Nashville

is sexy.

At Benchmark on 2nd

It's hard to know how many
more songs to stay for when
they know *every* song.

My glass is empty so
that may be a good sign.
"One more drink" he sings.

This is getting complicated.
On the teevee the Dodgers
are winning. Maybe I should

get out before I think too
much about California.
That state can wait its turn.

Addie is hyped up on sugar.
Can I get a hallelujah, they sing.
We may never leave this room.

Safe

I don't think I've seen
a single police officer in Nashville.
No one would dare.

NASHVILLE

DAY THREE

Cash Day

Fourteen years and one day.
We made it baby!

We dress in black and
prepare to meet the man

in the same color.

At Frothy Monkey

I
Addie isn't sure about that potato wedge.
It's a commitment she says, cutting it in half.
Though she's pretty sure she's going to
go in for the other half.

II
I've had so many
I'm sure my blood now
runs with biscuits.

Cash-ing In

We're both wearing Johnny Cash t-shirts
sitting across the street from a place called
Ca$hville about to head to the Johnny Cash
museum. Actually we're going to tour the
Ryman theater first, but that doesn't make
for as good repetition in poetry.

Also I'm concerned when we do get
to the Johnny Cash Museum that they're
going to try to up-sell us with a combo
ticket that includes the Patsy Cline Museum.
Always with the add-ons.

Sleeping Baby

Walking through the arcade between
4th and 5th streets, I want to tell the man
Excuse me sir I'm pretty sure your
baby is dead because it couldn't
possibly look that comfortable
while alive.

Attraction

They must be on the
Fall-off-a-golf–cart-in–the-
streets-of–Nashville Tour
I think as I observe this
seatbelt-less group
head up the hill.

Serendipity

We pass by a place called
Serendipity Labs and Addie
isn't sure she wants to
leave whatever they're doing
in there up to serendipity.

Healthcare

I see an ad that says
We sell shingles!
I wonder if they also
sell the cure.

The Ryman Auditorium –
Everyone Welcome
Everybody Come

I
The Violent Femmes
and Echo and the Bunnymen
both played here in July.
I already like it here.

II
I hand him the tickets and
Addie isn't quite in site so
he asks if someone else is
with me. *No.* I tell him.
I like to buy two tickets
just in case.

III
We stand in a building which
used to be the outside of the theater.
But then again everywhere used to
be outside.

IV
We enter through
what used to be
windows.

V
Our guide says if he hears a cell phone
he's going to answer it and he's feeling creative.
We might lose some friends on the way.

VI
This is the *mother-church*
of country music. The fifth home
of the Grand Ole Opry

VII
There's a hole in our guide's heart
remembering the teens he toured through –
All musicians who didn't know who
Ray Charles was.

VIII
Bluegrass music was born here.
They've long since cleaned up
the afterbirth.

IX
Everyone laughs when I ask
who Johnny Cash was.
My Johnny Cash T-shirt is
not lost on anyone.

X
When they renovated the Ryman
they pulled fifty gallons of gum
off the underside of the pews.
Our guide is glad he didn't
pull the short straw on that day.

XI
We hear *It wasn't God Who
Made Honky Tonk Angels*
sung by a group of angels.
We miss you Kitty Wells.

XII
Our guide has a personal vendetta
against Steven Tyler because of having
to screw the lightbulbs back in to the
vanity mirror in his dressing room.

XIII
The Ryman was
the Carnegie Hall
of the south.

XIV
If Lula Clay Naff thought she could
sell tickets, she would have booked the show.
The only color she cared about was green.

XV
Sarah Ophelia Colley Cannon
better known as Minnie Pearl
could kiss you within three feet
made a permanent impression
on me with just a *howdee!*

XVI
Hank Williams played *Lovesick Blues*
seven times during his debut at the
Grand Ole Opry. (Six of them were encores)
The audience loved every dAaaaAaaaDY...
He died at 29. Just once.

XVII
Nissan - innovation that excites
I think Nissan is overreaching
their expectations here about the
excitement level possible with
restroom hand dryers.

XVIII
Make a record at the Ryman
the sign says.

Again with the add-ons.

XIX
Reverend Samuel Porter Jones said
the conscience of Nashville is dead
into the skeptical ears of Tom Ryman
who became a believer and built
the Union Gospel Tabernacle which
eventually became the *mother church
of country music,* the Ryman, a place
started to save souls, became the
soul itself of Nashville.

XX
I still tear up some by the movie
when it was unclear whether they
we're going to save the theater or
tear it down, even though I am
standing in the saved theater.

XXI
A video tells us Nashville became one
of the nation's leaders in civil rights.
(And since then, based on our observations,
has exported all people of color to Memphis.)

XXII
It cost $35 to rent the Ryman
for a strictly religious meeting with no fire.
Add $10 for fire.

XXIII
To Samuel P. Jones
a reformed drunkard
every barroom was
a recruiting office for hell.
Quit your meanness
he would tell them all.

XXIV
Sarah Bernhardt played the Ryman twice
during two different "farewell" tours.

XXV
Lula Naff managed the Ryman
for 51 years, in the black while
bringing in the green. When she
finished, they called her
manager emeritus.

XXVI
The Opry moved away thirty-one years
after it opened here. The Ryman – the Opry's
fifth home. We'll see the sixth tonight.

XXVII
Howdeee! Minnie would say,
I'm just so proud to be here.
Watch it for yourself:
poetrysuperhighway.com/minnie

XXVIII
The sample guitars used for photo posing
are sadly out of tune until we get here
when we manage to get them to be only
slightly out of tune.

XXIX
I ask the woman taking the stage photos
If these will be available in the gift shop
or if they're just for personal use,
which makes her laugh and at least
not visibly judge me.

XXX
From almost-torn-down auditorium
to multiple *Venue of the Year* awards,
the *mother church of country music*
lives on.

XXXI
A book in the gift shop is called
Who Was Elvis Presley.
It's a hundred pages with huge print
that says *Do you seriously
not know who Elvis Presley is?*

XXXII
Addie wants to look in *Cafe Lula*
just to honor her but secretly
I think she wants a snack.

XXXIII
The sign that says *Taste the Ryman*
does not mean that I should start
licking the bricks.

Cashbound

I
We walk through Honkey Tonk Heaven
on the way to the Johnny Cash Museum.
They do not check your sins at the gates.

II
There's a store called Rock Bottom
right next to a boot store. They should
join forces and call themselves
Rock Bootem.

III
There's a Jimmy John's
down the street from the
Johnny Cash Museum.
They should combine forces
and open a Jimmy Johnny Cash's.

IV
The wind on 3rd street
almost blows our hair off.
It's quite windy today
Addie says
nonchalantly.

At the Johnny Cash Museum

I
In the cafe you can get
Folsom Prison Brew Coffee
And the tip jar has a big "Cash" on it.

II
"A Gunfight"
starring Kirk Douglas
and Johnny Cash:

*In Baja Rio they'll pay to
see a man kill a bull.*

*Today, they'll pay
to see a man kill
another man*

III
J.R. Cash's young 1940 face...
So full of the possibility
of never dying.

IV
*We'd rather catch a bullet
goin' over the wall than be
kept in this black hole.*
        ~inside the walls of Folsom Prison

V
I don't know what Johnny Cash song
Leonard Nimoy covered, but I want to know
so bad.

VI
I get to play with a mixer and I
turn down all the tracks except
for Johnny's voice because that's
all I need.

VII
In plain terms, Johnny was and is the North Star;
you could guide your ship by him.
        ~Bob Dylan

VIII
A couple of tag-lines from the Johnny Cash movie
Five Minutes To Live which was released in 1961
and then re-released with the title
Door-to-Door Maniac:

A woman's price drops fast as the time ticks away.

It could be your street...your house...your life!
When the bell rings...don't answer!

IX
Johnny's Guild —
A gift to the museum founder.
On display behind glass.
Will it make a sound again?

X
How cool would it be to
have a Johnny Cash t-shirt
I say while wearing a Johnny Cash
t-shirt in the Johnny Cash gift shop.

XI
I want to donate the t-shirt off my back
to the museum, for the sake of history.

At GooGoo Cluster

I
No one is sure if the samples
are free or if we're all about to
go to prison.

II
The faucet you need
once covered with free sample caramel
bubbles up like a volcano.

Water all over you,
and then you notice the small sign
"pull faucet upward slowly."

New idea:
Fix the faucet instead of
putting up a sign.

Just a Little

I cry everywhere in Nashville.
Apparently, I'm a little bit more country
than I thought.

More About My Eyes

I
One abbreviated license plate says
STDNT DRIVER which I see as
STUNT DRIVER. Either way I'm
proceeding with extreme caution.

II
An upside down sign says
Sidewalk Closed which I think
says the sky is closed.

III
At first I thought it was a fish tank
but on second look it's a big screen
TV showing baseball.

IV
I have 20/20 vision but all the
evidence points to me also having
20/20 visions.

Grazing

The waitress at Graze in East Nashville,
a vegan restaurant, asks if we want
separate checks. Our wedding rings
are visible but in this establishment
of tolerance, where pride flags hang
in the window, and a "No bigots"
T-shirt on her torso, nothing is to
be assumed.

Driving to the Opry

All of this used to be trees
or underwater or specs of
items still propelled by an
ancient explosion.

Spotted on the Way

Grand Ole golf carts
Opry Mills Mall
Opry Guest House
Grand Ole Navy
Grand Ole Dave and...
well just Dave
Buster was too young to include
and a Waffle House
in the distance between
several trees.

At the Grand Ole Opry

I
Why they don't call the shop at the Opry
The Shopry, I'll never understand.

II
If someone doesn't say *Howdeee!*
when the show starts, I want
everyone's money back.

III
Gravy - it's who we are.
It's a beverage.

In the south the tea is sweet
Just drink it

You don't have to eat the grits
It just comes with it.

IV
We're going to make an album together
As soon as we can find some money.
                ~ Emily West

V
He says playing here is like
forever being at church.
The circle is unbroken.

VI
These wipes were made for doers.

VII
WSM 650
We Serve Millions

VIII
Yes. You can get a *woo woo*.
In fact here are several.
(The woman behind me is
prematurely *woo woo-ing*.)

IX
The announcer is making announcements
between bands – anniversaries, birthdays, etc.
This is the first time I'm wearing pants in
a week. Please tell everyone, Mr. Announcer, sir!

X
I'm here for the music
not your patriotic bullshit.
So say the pledge of allegiance
on your Facebook page every day
if you want, but leave it out of
my Grand Ole Opry experience.
All of you, my ass.

The Opry Backstage Tour

I
The announcer got married a week ago
This tour is his honeymoon.

II
Other music has fans.
Country music has family.

III
They have eighteen dressing rooms –
One through nineteen
No number thirteen.
My Jewish superstition doesn't
know what to think.

IV
No alcoholic beverages
are served backstage

...anymore.

V
I'm in Roy Acuff's dressing room
Number One
thanks to his
open door policy

VI
A little country girl
eight years old by
my reckon, does
a solo line dance
on stage.

VII
The artists have to go
through security and
metal detectors
just like real people.

P.S. They also move their own cones
in front of their parking spots.

VIII
I'm sitting in Studio A which
used to be the *Hee Haw* corn field.
This country has been swelling up
inside me since 1975.

IX
Our guide disagrees with the Ryman guide
who said some *Nashville* tv show sets were built in LA.
I'd like them to arm wrestle to the death to decide the truth.

X
*The higher the hair
the closer to God.*

Goodnight, Nashville

Nashville, I was suspicious at the start
coming from Memphis where

the local currency is a smile.
But I've grown to like you.

I don't think I've wept this much
since New Orleans.

A good city makes the water come.
We've left things unsaid and undone.

A roster for the future.
More biscuit for my blood.

More honky for my tonk.
I'm driving away in the morning

the appeal of the brown water
across the border, what you call

whiskey, is what started this
whole thing. You did your part.

The circle is unbroken and
I'm standing in it.

ON THE WAY
TO LOUISVILLE

Time Zone Mad Dash
to Kentucky

The entire vacations is almost ruined
when we realize the Maker's Mark Distillery
in Kentucky, is in a different time zone
and that sacred beverage may be
an hour too far away. Praise the
bourbon friendly saints, the geniuses,
at Budget Rent a Car who tell us
we can pick up the car, whenever we want.

Forlorn Chicken

The forlorn chicken we passed
on fourth Street, on the way to breakfast
or really the human in the chicken costume
at least I think, it's been so long since
I've seen a live chicken...

Every intersection in Nashville

is one of those ones that at the right time
you can cross diagonally to the opposite corner,
at least all the good intersections.

Sorry to wake you boys

but you're going to need to
clear out of that elevator
before we get on, as dictated
by the laws of physics and
spatial dynamics, that is if
the lobby is your final destination.
If not, then I apologize for
the *sorry to wake you.*

A Geyser of Corvettes Shoots Out of the Ground

A sign advertising the Corvette Museum tells us
they have a sink hole exhibit. Every day at 3 o'clock,
like old faithful, they drive a corvette from every decade
right into that sink hole for the enjoyment of tourists
from all over the world. Later, at 5 o'clock, every day,
like old faithful, a geyser of corvettes shoots, like a rainbow,
into the sky, for the enjoyment of those who are
smart enough to stick around.

Things We Pass On The Way To The Maker's Mark Distillery

The Corvette Museum
The Kentucky Museum
Mammoth Cave
Horse Cave
A horse
Smith's Grove
Bowling Green
Abraham Lincoln's Birthplace
          and Boyhood Home
Barren Run Baptist Church
Flealand
Several *no passing* signs
The Kentucky Railway Museum
So much corn
Oh Kentucky, we didn't allow for
enough time to take in all
you have to offer.

At Maker's Mark

I
We cross time zone lines
in the middle of Kentucky
Whoever drew the time zone lines
had been to the distillery.

II
We stick our fingers in the mash
at the guide's suggestion.
I knew I tasted people's fingers
In my Maker's Mark.

III
Handcrafted labels and
bottles. It's one person's
job to cut labels all day.

IV
I want to taste my wife's
finger in a future bottle.

V
We can smell the Angel's share
where the barrels are.
They call it a *rickhouse.*

VI
Since I'm named Rick I assume
I'm entitled to a free barrel of whiskey.
Yes, Rick, the guide says
any barrel you can carry by yourself
is yours to take.

VII
Six-million barrels in Kentucky
for four million people –
Kentucky is ready for
the zombie apocalypse.

VIII
They make their bungs out of walnut.
Who doesn't, I think.

IX
Old marketing slogan:
*It tastes expensive
and it is.*

X
We need our own private
bourbon. *Rick and Addie Select*
seasoned with our fingers.
One barrel would last
well past our own lives.

XI
One woman's job is to
look at bourbon bottles as
they go by on a conveyer belt
just to make sure they're alright.

XII
At the very least
I want a private tasting
in the rickhouse.

XIII
I'm a rick-house
I'm mighty mighty
just letting it all
hang out.

XIV
They give smelling instructions
at the tasting...they say
when you smell
have your mouth open.
Oh, the things I thought
I knew how to do.

They say not to do the
Kentucky Chew. Just let it
sit on your tongue.

XV
Out guide drinks his *46* with ginger ale
which horrifies bourbon drinkers.
But he was raised Southern Baptist
and that's how he was taught.

XVI
They give us *cask strength*
at the tasting. This is an unpaid
endorsement for you to buy it.

XVII
They give us mint julep
at the tasting. This is an unpaid
endorsement for you to buy it.

XVIII
Connecting us with last summer
there's a Chihuly exhibit
outside of the tasting room.
Seattle. Kentucky. Forever.

XIX
I'm upset that most squirrels
don't believe that I'm on their side.

A NIGHT IN
LOUISVILLE

For Harlan Ellison

He had a mouth
and his typewriter screamed.
The city on the edge of forever
has its new mayor.

At the New Hotel

The elevators
have stopped
talking to us.

On the Way to Dinner

Ask me about my new cross-cultural
food concept combining a sloppy joe
and poutine to create the slopoutine.

Breaking News

I'm not sure where Addie is.
Either she's been kidnapped
or she's gone to the powder room.
More as the situation develops.

At Against the Grain Brewery and Smokehouse

They point out their old smoker.
It's okay I tell them
I don't smoke.

Main Street

We walk by the Murphy Elevator Company.
It never occurred to me I could have my own elevator.
Addie would like to interrupt this poem to tell me
I would need more than one floor.

Bourbon is not possible without water

says a sign outside of the now closed
Hillbilly Tea. Maybe they went out of business
because they forgot to add water.

Still on Main

I
It turns out the KFC Yum Center
is a concert venue and not a Kentucky Fried Chicken
turned Museum as I had been praying for.

II
The Humana Building on Main Street
has me convinced I don't have the skills
necessary to make a building.

At the 21c Museum Hotel Museum

I
The Sleep of Reason Produces Monsters
Yinka Shonibare MBE, 2008

And the owls make it impossible
to get anything done.

II
The Age of Enlightenment
Yinka Shonibare, 2008

Geometry is hard without a head...
And I suspect cartography too.

III
Addie feels like we've seen
Mrs. Surfboard's face before.

IV
Black Magic at the White House
Jeannette Ehlers, 2009

They can't evict you if you're translucent.
No matter how much noise you make.

V
Addie likes it in the
neon glow forest.

VI
Self-portrait as a Model Citizen
Wilmer Wilson IV, 2012

Covered head to Nashville with
I Voted stickers.

Tastefully, you can't see his
hanging chad.

Nightcap

I'm having an Elmer T Lee shot of straight bourbon,
expensive and rare to find, except the time our waiter
found it at a *Stop and Go.*

They will not stamp my Bourbon Trail Passport here
at the historic Seelbach Bar where presidents have stayed
and sipped, where the lobby staircase has a reputation of its own.

But with over one hundred and fifty bourbons available,
I am authorized to add my own travel visas.
He brings us the bottle so we can see Elmer.

It's the bartender's favorite to pour because of the way
the shape of the bottle feels in his hands. He displays a lot of trust
by leaving the bottle at the table.

At twenty-eight dollars a pour we feel a little like criminals.
Criminals like the ones who used the tunnels under this
building whenever they needed.

That was so long ago and, speaking of time, the ducks at
the Peabody feels like it was a long time ago. I'll never get used to
the passage of time.

A DAY IN
LOUISVILLE

Our Historic Hotel

Our hotel room is so tiny...
(*How tiny is it,* you say?)
It's so tiny, it fits on the tip
of a Louisville Slugger bat.

Our Historic Hotel

Our hotel room is so tiny...
(I can't hear you...)
It's so tiny, Ant Man himself
requested a larger room.

Our Historic Hotel

Our hotel room is so tiny
(Aighhhhhhh)
I don't have room to finis

Underneath Our Historic Hotel

There are underground tunnels
Capone and other ill-reputers
used leading from under our hotel
to the Federal Reserve Building
which have long been sealed up
but, which I want to see more than
a julep wants mint.

Coughing in a Lyft

If you use your car for ride sharing
you should also not use it for smoking.

Glancing at Menus for Dinner

One restaurant that we don't end up
choosing, offers a basket of livers.
Everything is better in a basket.

At the Louisville Slugger Factory and Museum

I
A giant Louisville Slugger sits outside
beckoning us to touch it like a Godzilla mezuzah
before we enter the museum

II
We miss the nub decorating exhibit
by ten minutes.

III
A sign asks *who should be the next mannequin.*
I'm hoping they pick me.

IV
Addie has decided she
will be the next mannequin
and is already posing.

V
A *lesser* wood is used to
make our souvenir mini bats.

VI
It takes forty-thousand trees to make
one season's worth of bats.

VII
All children here are
called *little leaguers.*

VIII
They started making bedposts
butter churns and doors.

IX
It used to take twenty minutes of
hand turning to make a bat.
The machines they use now do it
in thirty seconds.

X
The sawdust goes to make turkey beds.
Oh holistic tree, oh, gobble,
oh, sleep well turkeys.

XI
They make almost two million bats a year here
which is more than I need.

XII
The guide hands Addie a pink bat.
It's a bit typecasting but she loves it.

XIII
Free nubs!

XIV
Every home run I hit in the major leagues
was with a Louisville Slugger.
            ~Harmon Killebrew

XV
The Giving Tree

I'm sure if a tree had a preference
It would want to keep growing towards
the sky rather than be a door or bed post
or butter churn, or even a baseball bat
is what I have to say at the exhibit called
A Tree's Journey.

XVI
One exhibit is called *Reading a Bat.*
I wonder if they have open mics.

XVII
Addie does become a mannequin.
She doesn't care that I took the picture
ten minutes earlier, this is her calling.

XVIII
These free souvenirs mini bats
will protect us in the wilds of
Main Street as the bourbon infused
tourists approach us wanting
to interact.

XIX
I swing the Justin Turner bat
because I am from Los Angeles
and he has a beard suitable
for living in the forests where
the trees that made his bat
came from.

XX
The only man I idolize more than myself...
          ~Mohammad Ali on Hank Aaron

XXI
Bat room
Bath room
Be careful what
you do where.

XXII
Addie is storing her mini bat
in her batpack.

XXIII
Addie poses inside the
giant baseball glove.
She's quite a catch.

XXIV
It is not surprising to me that
you can buy baseball bats
in the gift shop.

XXV
The crack of the bat
is the heart of the game
is in italics here, but I'm not sure
if I came up with it, or if I saw it
quoted in the museum and
forgot to type in who said it.

XXVI
I almost weep at
the end of the film.
Almost. I miss Elvis.

XXVII
The 80 feet tall Louisville Slugger
rises in the air like an Eiffel Tower.
Can't find it? Just look up.

XXVIII
All of Louisville is a little bit on edge
as Addie walks the streets happily
attempting to balance her mini bat
on her finger up and down Main Street.

At the Evan Williams Bourbon Experience

I
They're not on edge that so many
people come into the place with
mini baseball bats.
(It's a different story when
everyone leaves the tasting
still with their bats.)

II
Is that a mini baseball bat
in my pocket or am I just
hiccup.

III
Evan Williams was a real person.

IV
You could spend whiskey just like money
back in the day.

V
They agreed no one would drink the whiskey
until after the meeting's business was over.

VI
Evan Williams wanted to make
more whiskey than anyone else.
And he wanted it to be the best.
(I'm glad he added that part.)

VII
Corn malt and rye or wheat
to Kentucky water
filtered through limestone
to mash
to distiller's beer
to low wine
to high wine
to barrels
to bourbon
to my mouth

VIII
There are five laws of bourbon.
I don't remember what any
of them are.

IX
Again, I'm inside a rickhouse
You're welcome everyone.

X
They say reusing a barrel
is like reusing a tea bag.

XI
They say all nations are welcome here
except Carrie Nation. (You'll have to
look her up to know why...what am I,
your Google?)

XII
Prohibition makes our guide nervous
and provides a clue to the identity
of Carrie Nation.

XIII
William Heavenhill looks like
a wild eyed human Sasquatch.
(No offense to his descendants
or the Sasquatch community.)

XIV
A nice warm Kentucky hug
travels down into my stomach.

XV
Athens Second Bourbon is described as
an *approachable* Bourbon.
I'll keep that in mind if I see one
on the street.

XVI
He describes an elevated tasting
as one in which you elevate your arm
before tasting, which is all the
elevation I can handle right now.

XVII
We bloom the bourbon
I'm still not sure what that means.

XVIII
After the tasting I'm ready to
smash things with my mini bat.

XIX
Photos on the wall —
the higher the pants,
the more excited they were.

XX
Good bourbon has nothing to prove
a t-shirt tells me. I've had a lot of bourbon
and am listening to t-shirts now.

XXI
A cocktail recipe book in the gift shop
calls for a hump of ice. I have found the
long-lost ice recipe of my dreams.

XXII
I see a three hundred and fifty dollar
bottle of bourbon inside a display case
and that's right where it stays.

XXIII
Every distillery does a honey whiskey
and a fire whiskey. (That's wisdom
from inside my Rick-house.
[I call my brain my "Rick-house" now.])

XXIV
The Whisker Dam* is like an
umbrella for your face. I'm not sure
that's interesting to you but I've had
a lot of high proof Bourbon so my
judgement about what to write down
is limited.

*A real product. Look it up at www.whiskerdam.com

XXV
I use the in-store iPad to sign up for the email list.
It's getting to the point where I have to scroll back
a lot of years when entering my birthday.

XXVI
The exit is one floor down.
I should not be operating stairs
in this condition.

Main Street

I ask Addie if she thinks the UPS guy
in front of Evan Williams Bourbon Experience
knows our UPS guy in Van Nuys.
I don't know if they have conventions
she says.

Main Street

We take to the streets of Louisville
with bourbon in our blood and
little mini bats in our hands.
It's getting all *Clockwork Orange*
up in this.

Hurrah!

I couldn't be more satisfied that *Heine* in *Heine Brothers Coffee* is pronounced the way it is.

Sobriety Test

Addie says she was just looking
at that woman eating a piece of bread
and that's why she ran into the metal barrier
and it's ME who's had too much bourbon?

I’ve had moo touch bourbon.

hahahahahahahahahahahahaha
hahahahahahahahahahahahaha
hahahahahahahahahahahahaha
hahahahahahahahahahahahaha
hahahahahahahahahahahahaha
hahahahahahahahahahahahaha
hahahahahahahahahahahahaha
hahahahahahahahahahahahaha!

Main Street

Although the song referenced earlier in this book says *stay on the sunny side*, we prefer to walk on the shady side of the street.

Main Street

The Central Bank Building
has two lighthouses on it.
They're just showing off.

At the Jim Beam Urban Stillhouse Because There Are So Many Empty Spots On Our Bourbon Trail Passport And We're Only Here For One Day.

I

I want to get inside the etching machine
and have my name etched into myself
in case I get lost and forget who I am.
(That could be the Evan Williams talking.)

II

They've got a bourbon bottle tree here.
I want the seeds.

III

A sign says *touch anywhere to begin*.
The store staff makes it clear they don't
like where I've touched.

IV

I see three glasses in front of me and
the sign promised *four*. I'm ready to
throw down with my bat self.

V

All bourbon is whiskey.
Not all whiskey is bourbon.
All whiskey is family.

VI

LBJ made Bourbon
America's national spirit.
Today our president makes
nothing but emptiness.

VII
Bourbon is at least 51% corn
they tell us
and 20% cob
I tell them.

VIII
They use alligator char wood
in their barrels. Thankfully,
this does not involve the usage
of real alligators.

IX
There are bourbon laws but
no one we'll tell me if there is
Bourbenomics.

X
I spent three days making up
the best way to spell
Bourbenomics.

XI
The smoked maple,
he assures us
is a *big boy*.

XII
They turn on the overhead
bottling line for me and I'm
like a kid in a bourbon store.

Fourth Street

The Fifth Third Bank
is on Fourth Street
which confuses
the fuck out of me.

I Don't Know Where This Was Written

The elevator doesn't talk
but we know what it's thinking.

At The Kentucky Museum of Arts and Crafts

I
A German Shepherd
A swim against the tide
A faster run
The tornado
Two wrestling cats
The burning forest
The dying wind
The lost ocean liner
Three felled trees

II
A wall full of
The Beatles *White Album* –
Step aside Pink Floyd.

Off Main Street

Corn Island is where it all began.
(The Louisville part of "all")

My Friend Julie

My friend Julie picks up ghosts.
She's done it twice now. *Tumps* them
from one plane of existence to the next.

She's done this with people too.
Odds are if you have a person or thing
that needs to move on, she's your person.

Don't ask though, she's not interested.
She has a past that involves adding a pickle.
Once I wore a sombrero to her birthday

party. I have no idea why I did that.
We sit for more hours than we should
be allowed, at a table surrounded

by red penguins. One penguin
was by request. The second a surprise
bomb in the photo.

The last time I saw Julie it had been
twenty years and she said *I don't think
it should be another twenty.*

We got it down to twelve or thirteen
this time. At our age it's hard to keep track.
We're narrowing the distance.

We're messing with the time zones.
We're proposing a future where
she stamps my passport all the time.

My friend Julie calls the highways
freeways and because of our shared
heritage, I'm on board with that.

My friend Julie dropped her ghost off
before dinner. She cleared all the spices
out of the kitchen. We laughed and laughed

at all our triumphs and failures. We caught
the tump up. *Tump* is a word that means
something. Trust her.

Windon'ts

For some reason
at the 21c Hotel
there are windows
that allow you to see
in and out of the bathrooms.
A layer of translucent water
and eyeballs, your only
hope for privacy.

As an aside to this whole experience

I'm fairly certain a whirlwind of corn should be called a cornado.

Fourth Street

Addie swims one last time
through the giant bourbon barrel
on fourth street and it's the cutest thing
Louisville has ever seen.

Our Historic Hotel

Our hotel room is so tiny
(say it wherever you are...)
It's so small, oh crap
you missed it.

Louisville

Louisville, which
I prefer to pronounce in
the original French

despite the
drawl draw of the locals
has fed me

batted me, asked
for my money in the streets
Bourboned me

beyond my
ability to bourbon.
Louisville

however
you say it, is
worth saying.

No-one Likes the Last Night of Vacation to End

I'd like to squeeze
one more poem
out of this last night.
Here it is.

A DAY SPENT
GOING HOME

Our Historic Hotel

Our hotel room is so tiny
(I can almost hear you..)
We put it in our carry-on
and flew back home.

Elvis seems like a hundred years ago

I hardly remember the faces of the ducks.
Martin Luther King, Jr. feels like
his lifetime ago. I recall being in his room.
Sun Studios. Are you really back there?
Did all that really happen? I don't even
remember coming up with the idea
of Nashville. How did I get here?
Mississippi River, Cumberland river
I need a river back in Van Nuys to
help me remember. No good town
would be seen anywhere without
its river.

Omelove

Addie is excited about the mushrooms
at the omelet station and says *mushrooms*
out loud. The only problem is he's preparing
my omelet and starts to add mushrooms.
This is what I signed up for when we got
married. Taking a mushroom for the union.
One soul, one flesh, one omelet.

Dead Luggage Walking

That last hotel hallway walk
The sound of the closing room door
The room you may never see again
The walk to the elevator
The elevator that doesn't speak
The trip down
The lobby
Pulling the luggage
The car
The city
left behind

James Elder of Kentucky, 1790

He serves our breakfast and
his family has been here since 1790.

He visited their graves and found
one with his name.

Seven generations later and it's him
who puts the coffee on our table.

James Elder of Kentucky.
A legacy.

The Great Gatsby

Since it was the only assigned book
I read in high school,

I'm in a heightened state
to be in this hotel, in this dining room

where Fitzgerald stayed, where he
set some of the book

where Jay Gatsby turned from an idea
into pages and pages of memory.

The Little Kentucky River

runs through the full size Kentucky
and, in any case, is not as little as our
tiny Louisville hotel room.

The Hog Wild Pig Crazy Bar-BQ

is more than I can handle at
this point in my life.

A Fly Off the Wall

I walk out of the *Love's Travel Stop* bathroom
in Sanders, Kentucky, with my fly as down

as it can be. When Addie points this out and
I try to convince her that's how the Kentucky gravity is.

No, that's just you, she replies will all her knowledge
of how me and physics collide.

Running Out of Time

As we get closer to Cincinnati
I pray they'll change the name of the city
to CincinAddie sometime in the
next thirty miles.

The Cincinnati, Ohio airport is located in the state of Kentucky.

This whole vacation has been a lie.

No sense gettin' stung by a bee during them last moments in Kentucky.

I'm not sure why
I was concerned about bees
at this point.

At the Cincinnati, Ohio Airport in the Great State of Kentucky

Half of the store called *Kentucky!*
sells *Ohio* merchandise. They should consider
renaming it *Cincitucky.*

Check In

The boy who checks us in
and since I'm approaching five decades

I can call him a boy, even with his job
and his beard, is much more excited

about our final destination than he is
about his daily choice. Cincinnati

or northern Kentucky. I tell him we're
just going home and that there's so

much more left to do on his ground.
Yeah but the sun he says, here on

one of the sunniest days in the south
mid-west. Isn't the sun always more

yellow in the other side of
the ticket counter?

On the Plane Home

I
I would like to visit Budapest
I tell the airplane magazine
in response to its article titled
"Visit Budapest". Send me a
paprika sample and we'll
seal the deal! I'm not as
interested in the shirts
designed to be worn untucked.
Sorry, airplane magazine,
you can't win them all.

II
Should I be nervous the pilot
just asked a child visiting the cockpit
where she was headed?

III
Now the magazine
wants me to believe
fish sauce is the
new vanilla.
No. Just no.

IV
We got upgraded to first class
but not in adjacent seats so I'm
already planning to convince
someone to move by shouting
across the aisle *Honey! How's*
your ganectagazoid? Is it
still contagious?

V
I'm on a plane.
The last time I was on a plane
it was one of Elvis'.

VI
This plane is
bound for L.A.
This plane.

VII
Out the window
I see Los Angeles is still here.
So that's one less thing
to worry about.

On the 405

On the way home
the sign that says *Lake Balboa*
I'm pretty sure says *Lake Bourbon.*

EPILOGUE

Epilogue

We picked up our son from camp today.
He looks older. He talks older.

Still doesn't like powdered sugar.
Doesn't remember how he got any

of the scabs on his legs. He says
I want to stay longer next year.

For a moment I'm excited about a future
window of time suitable for crossing the ocean.

But I see how tall I imagine he's become since
we saw him twelve day-long lifetimes ago.

By next summer, he'll be as tall as Elvis.
I'll never get used to the passage of time.

Rick Lupert will return in
The Tokyo-Van Nuys Express.
(May, 2020)

ABOUT THE AUTHOR

The author ascending to the biscuit throne in Memphis.

Three-time Pushcart Prize, and Best of the Net nominee Rick Lupert has been involved with poetry in Los Angeles since 1990. He was awarded the Beyond Baroque Distinguished Service Award in 2014 for service to the Los Angeles poetry community. He served for two years as a co-director of the non-profit literary organization Valley Contemporary Poets. His poetry has appeared in numerous magazines and literary journals, including *The Los Angeles Times, Rattle, Chiron Review, Red Fez, Zuzu's Petals, Stirring, The Bicycle Review, Caffeine Magazine, Blue Satellite* and others. He edited the anthologies *A Poet's Siddur: Shabbat Evening - Liturgy Through the Eyes of Poets, Ekphrastia Gone Wild - Poems Inspired by Art, A Poet's Haggadah: Passover through the Eyes of Poets,* and *The Night Goes on All Night - Noir Inspired Poetry,* and is the author of twenty-three other books: *17 Holy Syllables, God Wrestler: A Poem for Every Torah Portion,* (Ain't Got No Press) *Beautiful Mistakes, Donut Famine, Romancing the Blarney Stone, Professor Clown on Parade, Making Love to the 50 Ft. Woman, The Gettysburg Undress (Rothco Press), Nothing in New England is New, Death of a Mauve Bat, Sinzibuckwud!, We Put Things In Our Mouths, Paris: It's The Cheese, I Am My Own Orange County, Mowing Fargo, I'm a Jew. Are You?, Feeding Holy Cats, Stolen Mummies, I'd Like to Bake Your Goods, A Man With No Teeth Serves Us Breakfast* (Ain't Got No Press), *Lizard King of the Laundromat, Brendan Constantine is My Kind of Town* (Inevitable Press) and *Up Liberty's Skirt* (Cassowary Press), and the spoken word album *Rick Lupert Live and Dead* (Ain't Got No Press). He hosted the long running Cobalt Café reading series in Canoga Park for almost twenty-one years and has read his poetry all over the world.

Rick created and maintains *Poetry Super Highway*, an online resource and publication for poets (PoetrySuperHighway.com), *Haikuniverse*, a daily online small poem publication (Haikuniverse.com), and writes and occasionally draws the daily web comic *Cat and Banana* with Brendan Constantine. (facebook.com/catandbanana) He also writes the weekly Jewish poetry blog *From the Lupertverse* for JewishJournal.com

Currently Rick works as a music teacher at synagogues in Southern California and as a graphic and web designer for anyone who would like to help pay his mortgage.

RICK'S OTHER BOOKS AND RECORDINGS

Beautiful Mistakes
Rothco Press ~ May, 2018

17 Holy Syllables
Ain't Got No Press ~ January, 2018

A Poet's Siddur: Friday Evening (edited by)
Ain't Got No Press ~ November, 2017

God Wrestler: A Poem for Every Torah Portion
Ain't Got No Press ~ August, 2017

Donut Famine
Rothco Press ~ December, 2016

Romancing the Blarney Stone
Rothco Press ~ December, 2016

Professor Clown on Parade
Rothco Press ~ December, 2016

Rick Lupert Live and Dead (Album)
Ain't Got No Press ~ March, 2016

Making Love to the 50 Ft. Woman
Rothco Press ~ May, 2015

The Gettysburg Undress
Rothco Press ~ May, 2014

Ekphrastia Gone Wild (edited by)
Ain't Got No Press ~ July, 2013

Nothing in New England is New
Ain't Got No Press ~ March, 2013

Death of a Mauve Bat
Ain't Got No Press ~ January, 2012

The Night Goes On All Night Noir Inspired Poetry
(edited by)
Ain't Got No Press ~ November, 2011

Sinzibuckwud!
Ain't Got No Press ~ January, 2011

We Put Things In Our Mouths
Ain't Got No Press ~ January, 2010

A Poet's Haggadah (edited by)
Ain't Got No Press ~ April, 2008

A Man With No Teeth Serves Us Breakfast
Ain't Got No Press ~ May, 2007

I'd Like to Bake Your Goods
Ain't Got No Press ~ January, 2006

Stolen Mummies
Ain't Got No Press ~ February, 2003

Brendan Constantine is My Kind of Town
Inevitable Press ~ September, 2001

Up Liberty's Skirt
Cassowary Press ~ March, 2001

Feeding Holy Cats
Cassowary Press ~ May, 2000

I'm a Jew, Are You?
Cassowary Press ~ May, 2000

Mowing Fargo
Sacred Beverage Press ~ December, 1998

Lizard King of the Laundromat
The Inevitable Press ~ February, 1998

I Am My Own Orange County
Ain't Got No Press ~ May, 1997

Paris: It's The Cheese
Ain't Got No Press ~ May, 1996

For more information:
www.PoetrySuperHighway.com